# Macmillan Bible Stories

### LEVEL 1

# Moses in Egypt

Retold by
## CAROL CHRISTIAN

## MACMILLAN

First published 1996

Published by MACMILLAN EDUCATION LTD
London and Basingstoke
*Associated companies and representatives in Accra, Banjul, Cairo,*
*Dar es Salaam, Delhi, Freetown, Gaborone, Harare, Hong Kong, Johannesburg,*
*Kampala, Lagos, Lahore, Lusaka, Mexico City, Nairobi, São Paulo, Tokyo*

ISBN 0–333–63937–5

Printed in Hong Kong

A catalogue record for this book is available from
the British Library.

Illustrations by Ann Baum/Linda Rogers Associates

# How the Israelites became slaves in Egypt

Long ago, a Hebrew shepherd and his family came to Egypt from Canaan. His name was Jacob, but God gave him another name, Israel. So the people of his tribe were called the children of Israel, or Israelites.

At that time, Egypt's rulers were called Pharaohs. When the Israelites first came, the Pharaoh who ruled the country welcomed them. He gave them land for themselves and for their flocks. They stayed there and so did their children and grandchildren.

The Israelites lived in peace with the Egyptians but they were not like them. Many of the Israelites were shepherds and had large flocks of sheep. They worshipped one God, while the Egyptians worshipped many gods.

'We are God's special people,' they said.

One Pharaoh hated the Israelites. He said, 'There are far too many of these people in Egypt. They're getting much too powerful. Let's show them that we are their masters. We need slaves to work for us. Let's make the Israelites build our cities.'

Pharaoh's officers obeyed his orders at once. They made the strongest men and women into slaves. They gave them all the hardest work to do.

The Israelites worked in the fields. They dug clay and made bricks. They carried huge blocks of stone. They worked all day in the burning sun. The foremen were cruel and beat them if they didn't work hard enough.

But the Pharaoh still had a problem. Hard work didn't kill the Israelites. Every year there were more and more of them.

So he said to his officers, 'Kill every baby boy that is born to the Israelites. Don't allow a single boy child to live. If we let them grow up, they'll form an army and fight against us.'

He spoke to the Egyptian people. 'If a son is born to any of the Israelites, throw him into the River Nile. That is an order. If they have daughters, let them live.'

The Israelites were terrified. They tried to save their sons in any way they could.

# The baby Moses

An Israelite woman called Jochebed hid her baby
until he was three months old. Then, when she
couldn't hide him any longer, she made a basket
for him. She covered it with tar, so that no water
could get in. Then she wrapped her baby up and
laid him in the basket.

She said to her daughter Miriam, 'We'll hide him
in the tall grass at the edge of the River Nile. Then,
if soldiers ask us where the child is, we'll say, "He's
in the river"!'

They hid the baby in the tall grass, and his sister
Miriam stayed nearby to watch over him.

That evening, Pharaoh's daughter came down to
the river to bathe. Miriam was terrified when she
saw her. 'Dear God, don't let her find our baby!'
she prayed. 'This woman is an Egyptian, a member
of Pharaoh's own family!'

8

The princess saw the basket in the water and said to her maids, 'Do you see that basket in the tall grass? I wonder what's in it. Go and get it. Bring it to me.'

When the maids brought the basket, and opened it, the baby began to cry.

Miriam, who was watching, caught her breath. 'Our baby's going to die!' she thought. 'Every day the Egyptians throw baby boys into the River Nile!'

However, the princess looked down at the baby and smiled. She felt sorry for him. She lifted him out of the basket and held him in her arms so that she could see him better.

'Oh, look!' she said to her maids. 'It's one of the Israelite babies! I think he's hungry.'

Miriam was listening. She approached the princess and asked politely, 'Shall I find an Israelite woman with milk in her breasts to feed him for you?'

'Yes, child,' said the princess kindly. 'He's a fine baby boy. I don't like to hear him cry.'

Miriam went home and told her mother, 'Pharaoh's daughter came down to the river to bathe and is holding our baby in her arms!'

Jochebed was terrified. 'What's she going to do to him?' she cried.

'She wants someone to feed him,' said Miriam. 'And I agreed to find someone. She won't let him die.'

Together they hurried back to the river.

'Take this child and feed him for me,' ordered the princess. 'Then, when he's older, bring him to me. I shall call him Moses and bring him up as my son.'

So Moses grew up in the royal palace and received a good education. He learned all the things that a young Egyptian prince learned.

However, he knew that he was an Israelite and he felt sorry for the Israelites he saw around him. Every year their lives became harder.

## Moses leaves Egypt and goes to the land of Midian

One day, when he was a young man, Moses went out to watch his people at work. An Egyptian foreman struck one of the Israelite workers a cruel blow. Moses was angry and he struck the Egyptian. He struck him so hard that the man died. Moses hid his body in the sand.

'Pharaoh will kill me if he learns about this,' he thought. 'And the Egyptians will hate our people more than ever.'

He left Egypt at once and escaped to the land of Midian, in the Sinai Peninsula.

Now Jethro, the priest of Midian, had seven daughters. One day they went to a well to get water for their father's sheep.

While they were there, some shepherds came and tried to drive the girls away. They wanted to get water for themselves. But Moses was sitting nearby. He stood up and chased the men off. Then he helped the girls to give water to their sheep.

When the girls told their father, Jethro said, 'Where's the man now? Did you leave him at the well? That wasn't friendly. Invite him to come and eat with us.'

He made Moses welcome, for Moses was a fine young man. He said to him, 'We're glad to meet you. Stay with us for a while.'

Moses couldn't return to Egypt while Pharaoh was alive, so he stayed with them for many years. He married Jethro's daughter Zipporah and they had a son. Moses became a shepherd and looked after his father-in-law's sheep.

# The burning bush

One day, when he was alone with the sheep on the slopes of Mount Sinai, Moses saw a fire. When he went near, he saw that a bush was burning. But it was a strange fire, for it didn't destroy the bush.

While he was wondering about this, he heard his name, 'Moses! Moses!' A voice was calling to him. It came from the burning bush! Slowly, he approached.

'Don't come any nearer,' said the voice. 'And take off your sandals, for you are standing on holy ground. I am the God of your ancestors, Abraham, Isaac and Jacob.'

Abraham was Jacob's grandfather and Isaac was his father. The nation of Israel began with them.

Moses took off his sandals. He pulled his head cloth over his face, because he was afraid to look at God.

God said to him, 'Moses, my people in Egypt are suffering. I have heard their cries and I have come to save them. I shall give them the land of Canaan, a land full of milk and honey. Go and tell Pharaoh to let my people go. Then lead my people out of Egypt.'

'Lord, how can I possibly do that?' cried Moses. 'Pharaoh and his officers will kill me.'

'A new Pharaoh is ruling Egypt now,' God told him. 'All the men who wanted to kill you are dead. And I shall be with you. When you bring the people out of Egypt, you will all worship God together here on this mountain.'

Moses couldn't believe his ears. 'Lord, I'm only a shepherd,' he said. 'I'm not the Israelites' leader. If I say that God sent me, they'll want to know his name. What shall I tell them?'

God said to Moses. 'I am who I am. That is my name. Tell them that the God of Abraham, Isaac and Jacob sent you.'

'They won't believe me,' said Moses.

Then God asked him, 'What are you holding in your hand?'

'My shepherd's staff,' answered Moses.

God said, 'Throw it on the ground.'

So Moses threw his staff on the ground and it turned into a snake. Moses backed away from it. He was astonished.

'Grab it by its tail,' said God. When Moses grabbed it, the snake turned into a staff again.

God showed Moses other signs. 'The Israelites will believe you when you show them these signs,' he said. 'They will know that God is with you.'

'Oh Lord, I'm not a good speaker,' said Moses. 'I can never find the right words to say. I'll never persuade the people to follow me.'

'My son, I made you. I shall put words in your mouth,' God said to him. 'You will know what to say.'

However, Moses still protested. 'Please send someone else, Lord. Don't send me.'

Then God got angry with Moses and his excuses. He said, 'Your brother, Aaron, is a good speaker. He will speak for you. He is coming to meet you and will be very glad to see you. You can go to Pharaoh together. I shall be with you. But you must take your shepherd's staff. You will need it for the signs.'

Moses went back to his father-in-law, Jethro, and asked him, 'May I return to Egypt to see my family?'

Jethro answered, 'Go in peace.'

## Moses returns to Egypt

Moses took his wife Zipporah and his son and set out for Egypt. And Aaron heard God's call and met him at Mount Sinai. They hugged and kissed each other. Then they went on into Egypt to talk with the leaders of the Israelites.

Aaron spoke for Moses. When he showed the Israelites God's signs, they believed him.

'God has seen the suffering of his people,' they said. 'Let us worship him.' And they bowed their heads and worshipped God.

# Moses and Aaron speak to Pharaoh

Moses and Aaron went to Pharaoh and said to him, 'The God of the Israelites has spoken to us. He wants his people to go and worship him in the wilderness. The journey will take three days. He has sent you this message: ***Let my people go***.'

Pharaoh couldn't believe his ears. 'Is your God giving me orders?' he shouted angrily. 'I don't take orders from him. And the answer is NO. I won't let your people go.'

'Listen to me, Moses and Aaron,' he continued. There are more Israelites than Egyptians in this country now. They do all the hard work. You can't take them away from their work for three days! We need them here.'

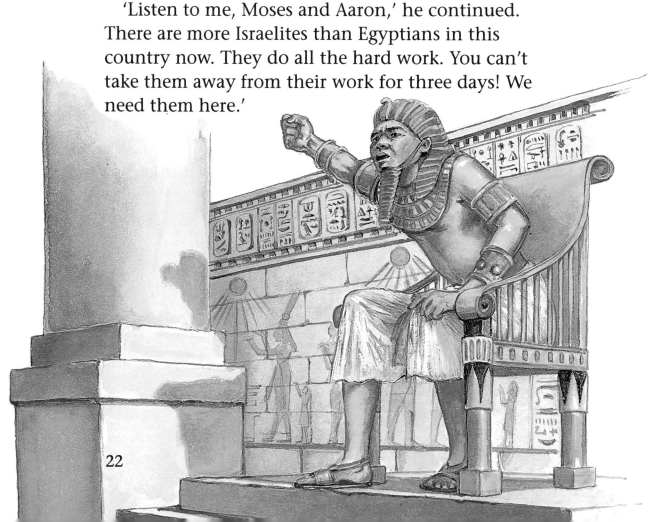

He was so angry that he said to his officers,
'Don't give the Israelite slaves any more straw to
make their bricks. They can find their own straw!
But see that they make as many bricks as they
made before. Beat them if they don't. They're lazy.
They want to leave their work and go into the
wilderness to worship their God!'

The leaders of the Israelites said to Moses and
Aaron, 'We're suffering more than ever. God will
punish you for this.'

Then Moses said to God, 'How can I make
Pharaoh listen to me? Even the Israelites don't
believe me. Why don't you do something?'

But God said, 'I will rescue my people, I promise.
Now go back to Pharaoh and tell him so. Repeat
the message: **Let my people go**.'

# God shows Pharaoh signs of his power

Then Pharaoh said to Moses and Aaron, 'Prove that God sent you. Show us a sign.'

So Aaron threw his staff on the ground and it turned into a snake.

Then Pharaoh sent for his magicians. When they came, they threw down their staves, which also turned into snakes. But Aaron's snake ate up the other snakes.

'Any magician can perform that trick,' said Pharaoh.

# God sends ten plagues

Then God said to Moses, 'Pharaoh goes down to the River Nile in the morning. Go there, too, and take your staff. Tell Pharaoh to let my people go. If he refuses, show him the second sign.'

So Moses and Aaron met Pharaoh on the banks of the River Nile. Moses said, 'God sends you this message: *Let my people go*. If you don't let them go, he'll turn the River Nile into blood.'

Then Aaron struck the water with his staff and it turned to blood. But Pharaoh sent for his magicians and they performed that trick, too. Now the people of Egypt had no clean water to drink.

A week later Aaron caused all the frogs in Egypt to leave the rivers. They came into the houses and kitchens and baking ovens. There were frogs in every house.

Once again, Pharaoh's magicians performed the same trick. But the people hated the frogs and the magicians didn't know how to get rid of them. Pharaoh hated them, too, because they got into his palace and into his bedroom and into his bed!

So, at last, Pharaoh sent for Moses and Aaron and said, 'Get rid of the frogs and then I'll let your people go and worship their God in the wilderness.'

But, as soon as the frogs returned to the rivers, Pharaoh forgot his promise.

Now the Egyptian people were really suffering. God sent one terrible plague after another down on them.

The first plague was when the water turned to blood.

The second plague was when the frogs left the rivers.

The third was a plague of gnats, which bit the people and made them itch, so that they scratched and scratched and scratched.

The fourth was a plague of flies, which got all over their food and spread disease.

Then Moses went to Pharaoh and said, 'God says: *Let my people go*. If you refuse, he'll send another terrible plague. All the Egyptians' horses and sheep and cattle will get sick and die. Only the Israelites' animals will remain healthy.'

That was the fifth plague. The animals died but Pharaoh didn't let the people go.

Then God said to Moses, 'Take ashes from the fire and toss them up towards heaven. A storm of dust will spread through the land. Painful boils will break out on the bodies of all the people and their animals.'

That was the sixth plague. Pharaoh's magicians couldn't do anything because they were suffering, too. They had painful boils all over their bodies.

Then terrible storms destroyed the crops of the Egyptians.

After that, there was a plague of locusts. The locusts ate up everything that remained, every blade of grass and every ear of corn.

Those were the seventh and eighth plagues.
Last of all, the sun disappeared from the sky and the whole land was in darkness.

Each time God sent a plague down on his people, Pharaoh promised to let the Israelites go. Each time he changed his mind. The Egyptians begged him to send the Israelites away, but he never did.

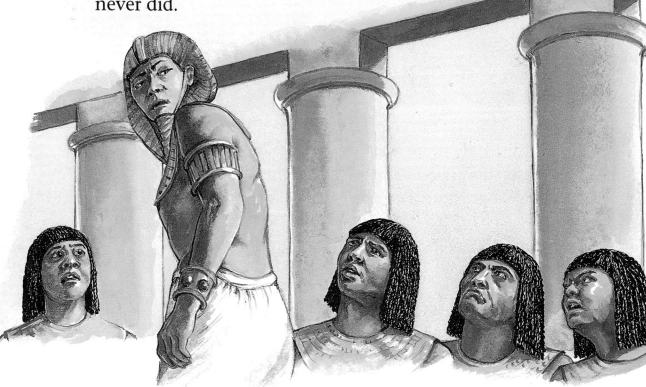

Finally God told Moses, 'I shall send one more plague. Then Pharaoh himself will beg you to leave his country. I shall come among the people at night and kill the first-born child in every family, from the highest to the lowest. I shall do the same with the animals. Pharaoh's first-born child will die. But not a single child of the Israelites will die.'

Moses warned Pharaoh, but still he did not let the people go.

# The Israelites get ready to leave Egypt

Then Moses told the Israelites, 'Get ready to leave Egypt. This is what God wants you to do. On the fourteenth day of the month each family must kill a lamb. Mark the doors of your houses with the lamb's blood. Then roast the lamb for your dinner.'

That night, the Israelites got ready to leave Egypt. Each family ate a meal of roast lamb and unleavened bread. They ate every bit. Nothing was left over.

At midnight, God passed through the land of Egypt, and killed all the first-born children. There was loud crying everywhere in the land, for someone was dead in every Egyptian house.

But God passed over every house that belonged to the Israelites, because the door was marked with blood.

That was the first Passover night. Even today, the descendants of the Israelites celebrate that night of the year with a special feast of roast lamb and unleavened bread.

# The Israelites escape from Egypt

When Pharaoh heard the cries of his people, over their dead children, he sent for Moses and Aaron. It was still night.

'Go!' he said to them. 'Take your families and your sheep and cattle, your gold and silver and whatever you have, and get out of Egypt! Go and worship your God.'

33

So the Israelites gathered up everything they had and left their homes. There were six hundred thousand of them, not counting the children. The Egyptians urged them to hurry before God killed the rest of them.

And Moses carried with him the bones of their ancestor Joseph, the son of Jacob. This was four hundred years after Joseph's death.

God led the children of Israel out of Egypt. He went ahead of them in a pillar of cloud by day and in a pillar of fire by night.

Even then Pharaoh changed his mind. His people started to say, 'Now that the Israelites have gone, we have no slaves. Who will work for us?'

Pharaoh decided to go after the Israelites and bring them back. He chased after them with six hundred chariots of war and all his soldiers. He caught up with them at last on the shores of the Red Sea.

When the Israelites saw Pharaoh and all his soldiers, they cried out to Moses, 'Did you bring us from our homes to die out here in the wilderness? We'd rather go back and work for the Egyptians!'

# God saves the Israelites

Moses said, 'Don't be afraid. Stay where you are. God will save you. You'll never see the Egyptians again.'

And God said to Moses, 'Lead the children of Israel forward. Hold out your hand over the sea to make a path for them. They will walk through the sea on dry land.'

When Moses held out his hand, a strong wind swept across the sea and blew the water up like a wall on either side. And the people walked through the sea on dry land.

Then Pharaoh's soldiers, with their horses and chariots, charged after the Israelites into the Red Sea. But Moses held out his hand again. This time, the water fell back, and closed over the heads of the Egyptians.

Pharaoh, his soldiers, and their horses and chariots, all drowned in the Red Sea that day. Not one of them remained alive.

But God saved the children of Israel. They came out of the Red Sea free people, not slaves. And, when they saw the Egyptians lying dead on the sea shore, they sang God's praises with thankful hearts.

And Moses led them on into the wilderness, towards Mount Sinai, to worship God there.

**Macmillan Bible Stories**

*Level 1*

**Adam and Eve**

**Noah**

**Jonah**

**Moses in Egypt**

**Jesus is Born**

**The Good Samaritan** *and*
**The Wise and the Foolish Bridesmaids**


*Level 2*

**Joseph**

**Ruth**

**When Jesus was a Boy**

**Jesus begins God's Work**
> *including the baptism of Jesus, the temptations, the draught of fishes, the wedding feast at Cana, the healing of the lame man, the blessing of little children and the feeding of the five thousand.*

**Lost but Found**
> The Lost Sheep
> The Lost Coin
> The Prodigal Son

**Jesus Dies and Lives Again**